For Vanessa

Nice to hear you

Alex W.

MAY

A W Singerman

Singerman & Company

Published by Singerman & Company 2011

First published in Great Britain in 2010

ISBN 978-1-4457-8138-9

www.williesingerman.com

for Cecilia

"External reality's too small, too unambiguous and too truthful to contain what there is inside a single man"

- Franz Kafka

MAY

A W Singerman

MAY

Contents

7.05.10 (Out of Office)

In Dialogue

What can I say?

Good question.

Worked

A title is something
you can believe in

the way you see
a new air
or outfit,

a certain gait,
opened doors,

promotions

What is Poetry?

Time
in no time

*

Not standing
still nor slowing
down

Just out of here

Over there

*

The ideal

Of silence

Before you

Breaking News

The reporter reveals
there is trouble
down under.

What an ego!

High Definition

World is easily transformed.

Did my heart just flutter
or shudder. The page is

frozen. My eyes get caught
sniffing my sleeve across
the back to back screens.

*

What you call
Absolutely ages

I call the present.

What you see
As a gift

I know as curses.

*

The system asks me
to choose expressions.

I am having trouble
processing

the ability not to multi-task.

Mind on
umbilical cord
or the phantom of

I shiver.

Does it mean something
or just the air

conditioning?

*

After a while, I suppose, it stops feeling
like a performance, but that is far from
making it real

*

No centre parts
on the fringe
of reason -

Not *my* voice

Obviously!

*

Own up.

OK, I did it.
I wrote the poem that tore the world apart.

*

Thank you
for ordering

The consequences

Look what's bouncing back -
that critical glue.

Do you peel it off
or paste over it

with praise
or prayers

*

As soon as you dwell
on other problems

you are released

*

Controlling an addiction
means making the most
out of it.

Easy now, you are stepping
on your shadow

if the light is behind you

*

At my level
you are side by side
with technology

which is why the ones
who switch us on and off
want us to feel superior.

9.05.10

Suddenly strange to me
my life appears
apart from all I have

the deafening voice of my thoughts
of the thing, i emphasise, thing
that thinks (thinks) it is in charge
((my thigh vibrates in time with eardrum))
(((an association is made)))
((an association is made with the association))
(translated as: I do not want to be disturbed)

My how strange this voice in my ear is to me
((another buzz - temptations - some wilderness))

but I was saying something sometime back
that must have been aiming at

well things have changed now
i am erratic like that

to be honest this is just a joke

The End

In second place comes Richard in the race
and he kicks himself for not cheating
or perhaps simply being The Best.

But I am way back in 8th Place
or the E Team, Class 4, or
behind my bedroom door
with the desklight on,
keeping score.

It didn't seem like it was up
to me, what I could do, but Life,
these days, does that to you,
beats it into you that you are
responsible (solely) for what
you become
                              but how far
does that take us? I know
there is a lot to see (a lot
of sea) how the flower
created the flea, but from way
back, I plea, it could be worse.

The Murder

It was in his third year of being
a writer in particular that he got
the notion that to understand,
he would have to kill.

By then he had swallowed enough opiates
to have pasted over the house rules
hastily scrawled on the walls of his
living room (Do you mind?) which was,
of course, invisible to him like everyone else.

Prostitutes were the obvious candidates
but he had known a few and knew
that they were simply desperate too
(finding it hard getting by
in a dying industry.
Dying of course in millions
of small ways, while changing
name, changing image.

And there used to be these things
people knew as sins, but I wasn't

in that world so obviously,
goodness being subtle so often.

Now I struggle so long
with the deafening voice
which debates every definition
every distinction and cannot
simply handle right and wrong

because they look like left and right
in the mirror inside a mirror
reflecting a mirror.

He said things like that, cryptic,
disturbing, but he was convinced
it wasn't true, it wasn't real

but what is this if not something
added to the world, yes I give you
myself I give away myself, for me
and the rest is up to you.

Prone to all sorts of things
the two continued to fight it

out on the page, while the carrier
simply typed and was puzzled by what
they (How many?) were saying.

Shoosh! Get on with it.

Answer Message

some peace

the inner wholeness
is a brief
insight
into the chaos
inside
and apart
of me

dreaming on

funny what goes out of fashion
thinks the green jumper
across the 8th sea

how did that
get there

You find yourself
unable to find
yourself. You find
out that yourself
is only for you.
You find in
that you're finding
something you thought
you'd lost (a blanket
for example. It's been
keeping you cold) and if
you had it here now
you know it would not
exist. You see, what
you see is difficult
to see, but what remembers
you has a more powerful force.

Memory

It’s a hard job
when you think
about it.

Humans being
so needy.

I’ve got a lot
to doubt.

Who do you think
was speaking there?

Not someone playing
a game.

You have to explain it first.
The rules.

I. When the voices arrive
take off your hat
and stay indoors.

II. Listen.

III. Make the wrong decision.

Those were the ones I was given
at the top of the mountain
hidden behind the clouds.

It became a craze.

People started making up rules

left, right and centre:
you can’t stand there
stop singing
leave me alone when i have to be alone

knock

oh oh

It sounds simple
because it's true -

different things
come out
different
          places

.

Do you remember
                    whoever you are
                                        how we measured
ourselves

in unknown feelings
                    which is why
                                        we do nothing but be

.

This is the way
I went
and am going

though all I have is every present

.

still it's continuous still it's continuous

Not that I
saw any of this
coming

.

Don't be absurd
says someone trained
in logic.

With good reason,
says he, implying
another sheet of
complexity, tissuethin
and probably
well worn.

.

That's how this ends
after I took off Jimmy's
heart felt hat, and see you
tomorrow, of course. New.

A Break

Supposedly, you take it
(putting the emphasis
on the "wrong" syllable)
this break which
is seen as
desirable.

But people live
in many ways,
at least two,
so different

it's hard to speak
to anyone but yourself

even in company we are
made up and distracted,
invented and connected
like the physics of poetry.

I Believe He's Gonna Loose His Mind

I have a theory
about mistakes
but spilling
waves of wax
might unclose
that other I.

.

Again then
my right hand
is always right.

.

Not like that
you dirty bastard

Unclean!

Look.

His rotten father

leads the parade.

.

I had a dream or

just as easily,

I had a dream, or

(just as easily)

a dream had me.

But I forgot

all about it.

13.05.10

From this rooftop
the tree reflected
on the reservoir
reminds me of myself

.

I know that we speak the truth
when we are saying nothing,
but I want to give the wind
a face, the sun a palm,
the moon some room

.

Traces, traces, traces

the word brought over
from a poem in a dream
that made perfect sense
over there, where it
stood me against a wall

and everything is repeated
in reality, reflected
into consciousness
once you look, remember
and remind yourself
there is no solid line

Secret

You can't come close

You have an idea but no idea if it's the right idea

It's exciting, in a disturbing way

It's disturbing, in an exciting way

Someone hands you a letter.
All the words are in a language
you don't understand.

The language doesn't exist
you think. You start
to read. It makes sense.

Someone asks you what
it is about.

You tell them
I don't know.

Time Takes A While

The way I see it
is unique, just like
the way you see it.

So it is not that
unique.

On the other hand sits
a "bad dream" you left
stranded on an island
of dark stars (hear them?)

How so, asks a stranger
who is not a stranger.

He's got my number
so I tried to change it.

Now my word is against his
wall, my arrow. Let's smooth
this out: what matters

is what is

around us

Boxes

The only time I can get going
is when I finally have to
get going. There is something
trapped inside me that takes revenge
and dresses it up in the cloak
of life. Now these are big things
I know they may not be for me
to handle (my gloves are so thin)
but but but I am hoping we all argue
like this so come on, take me on.

I believe in no camera
apart from one
that can light this

up or down or any
way you have it
in yourself

each stroke
of the timeless clock
sings like the bird
confined in this.

I am never alone
as long as I can think
of you and reach out
with a phantom branch
that begs –

stay with me

.

The lover's heart is tickled.
The scholar's throat puts on its boots.
The professor thinks about hiding places.

This is
obviously

connected
to nothing

I can explain.

Since K stands for D
and the sea is an automobile
all is well, surely

all is well.

Thrown

I am going on
for no reason

yet my shoulders shiver
the sun delivers itself
elsewhere for another
day. I would wait
on the moon
but who would reach me

and if that happened well
there'd be all
kings of outcome.

So nevermind the messages
I will leave off soon

the clock hints
this is inevitable

and such is life

who knows what
it means

14.05.10 (day)

I do not know what I contain
beyond these nebulous senses,
defences and attacks. My heart
trips in its thorny wonder
round the same route, over
& over

.

Give me a
Show me some
Tell me this

Truth on the skyline.

.

And from the rooftop he cried
I shall follow that floating
fagend. But he had the key
still warming in his pocket.

.

Sure enough
these might not give you much

too few flowers and the rain
is about it. Moreunder

But you've seen the sun right
and the moon is a snooze
in the ballpark. The pond
spills out with poltergeist
while I'm doing the crosscountry.

.

Where were we
nobody asked
and quite right
it is wrong
to feel good
about bad
and viceversa.

.

You made me
wonder
hopelessly
in the hope
of hope
wandering
how you made me

It is trying

you work for

some company

that does not exist

a clear statement

follows a twist

behind the guards

of the heart

(of the heart?)

Inside The Actor's Temple

Such strange religion.

Love

played out

in all its exhausted emptiness

as a flower blooms

into flames

inside me bursts

in vain

name only

we repeat

our

our

selves

selves

my answer is a question to you

Searching for a link
to the unbroken past
where this i recurs
without the rhyme,
the reason that stands
taller than this
blankeyed statue.

.

My eyes were on your tongue
which sung nothing, glorious
unintelligible. Your back completes
the headboard, I am still
holding on, dear life, do not
disrupt me as I cling
to our reflection of everything.

Notes of perfume.

The room is cold.
Eyes are old.

My sighs,
my size

.

Vision of the bus
in colour with background,
a sense of being hit
impending

the sound drifts... this ocean
of traffic continues

my eyes searching the shapes
for something recognisable
to unfold

but the letters from outside
wear strange faces, maybe
masks, armour, who am I
to know

this is the desperation
of communication impossible.

The old man in me smiles.

14.05.10 (night)

My belongings
have been hanging
around, waiting
to be boxed.

But doing, doing,
doing stuff
the plot
of this ghostly being
has got old.

We swore we were hatching
as if our curses could crack
the shells we were locked in.

Surely the key on the tree
has meaning, but then
again. The heat keeps
freezing us, naked
in the garden
the ropes
the rocks
the waves

Did you
hear?

Here? Here
nothing happens.

(Surely)

Only when every element accumulates
does it appear like something was made.

Supposing my voice
truly broke, I would
tap you on the shoulder
and tell you everything.

.

Whoever
whatever
ever
you are

.

Bring it back
down, the cliffs
are where the world
is rearranged - should you
be compelled, say a spell
like a lifetime.

.

Stranded shells
change their hairstyles
according to magazines
shot out by mysterious
news agents.

I am spy remember, but not
on you. Unless you happen to be
a set of keys. The door, you
saw it swinging, your ring
caught in the letterbox
engraved with my grandmother's
message: Don't Forget.

.

In the hall there was a sign
of someone scratching his head
that bubbled (like the woodpipes
I blew from the radiator, the hard
sweeties, the ragged blue rug
looking like the fur of some
kindly monster) "Every time I forget
something, I forget it, and remember."

But those were not the words.

.

Pa'an?

The doctor spotted her
hobbling into the car
on the steep hill.

Just a little shaky
on my pins, said
our granny
who was once
little Zuzie in Hungary.

.

Don't Forget?

I think it was
Remember Keys.

Keep the heid
were his last words
to his firstborn son

who he would sometimes
mistake me for, in name
at least, and as I wandered

the beach, far off
beneath the cliffs,
that lucky old sun
on my orangutang arms,
I was sure I was

David, the wandering
Jew, cast ahead.

Archetypes, of course, another me
sucks an imaginary pipe, exhaling
an assurance so temporary as to be
utterly meaningless.

.

And this moment?
Well, that's it.

How did I do?

Sirens. Steady flow. Endless.

I begged my muse
to sing a song,
my muse complied
I played along.

I played along
& learned the song,
my muse complained
I played it wrong.

I went along
still playing the song
& came up short.

I am too young
for this & too
old. My walking
stick has withered
into a pacifier.

Dummy! Give me back
my teeth
so I can tear
another piece
of green cloud

.

your eyes pop
your ears drop
your tongue rocks
round your sandcave throat

.

Back into a frame
your eyes cannot

make out the image
of your flashing eyes.

Trapped here & there
at once. Forever?
We can only hope.

Thing after thing after thing until
something breaks - wait

what are you
asking
"big questions"
floating effortlessly
on the strings of their answers.

.

Why not wings
or weight?

You see
in another
universe
you might
hold them

but this is what we have:
the familiar thump
of another last line.

Oddballs

A disembodied dog
walks about
with a sly grin.

Surely not.

.

The policeman receives
his new face & wears
his helmet with pride.

Or so it seems.

.

The bear has given up
(on the beat?)

The entire animal kingdom
sell their souls
for human blood.

Because it tastes that good.

.

All I am doing
is trying
to buy bananas
with a catchphrase.

Slippery, isn’t it, goes Cinderella.

15.05.10

Life is lived in my head
all of this is creation
recreated like a ceremony
for a cemetery where words
wait to come back to life

.

Nobody said my head belongs
to me, but I must have heard
it somewhere. Moving on
the teacups gather in the corner
of my vision and they can hardly
contain the entrails of the dragon.

.

But I am supposed to be serious
about this, meaning absolutely
certain that the absolution
has been fully certified.

.

Tie it all together.
Wrap this present up
with string & swing
something toward you

This is
what happens
when you cannot
express yourself.

.

That leaf sure did seem
new, but then again (as I
always say) so was the fridge
full of Polish beer & my feet
changing direction of CCTV.

Gulps of beer
turn into red wine
to sweeten

This heart, I cry
I can't get over it.

.

So much for the mountain
back there, I never got
quite close enough, I fire
at will, who says

.

An atmosphere emerges
as the sky deepens.

Rinse the feathers
out your hair
and get your insides
a bottle of bubbles.

So what
depends

on so much.

Chicken. Etc.

- What do you call this, said the inspector.
- I don't know, I said.
- I see.

.

We are travelling through space on the back of an
interplanetary magnet.
When we hit Mars, it will undoubtedly explode.
I for one am glad I snuck
a green marker pen aboard.

.

Did you see that, says Jimmy the Golden Retriever.
I see someone waving from the fringes of the dark.
I play dumb.
Jimmy says he must have fallen into a black hole.
You are a black hole, I tell him.

No I can't
do it, no
I can't do
it, no I
can't do it

.

Am I moving
closer or
further

heart clenched
fist knocks

You packed up

.

Gone to some
damp cave

grey sky

lowers down

.

can't leave your body
for a minute, even tho
one contains
past present & future

18.05.10

I Make My Piece

It is important that you
wake up - that you may be
more free to make sense
without sense but it's noted
only on the thinnest

My it takes you
so long
to say hello
at a thought
rotted & indifferent.

You need more UMPH
I mean euch I mean
SHOOSH I mean
you know

No-one stands up and says
what is the meaning of this

Of course it is

Important Notice

Not one tiny little speck
of anything else
will do.

.

Something wrong?

Perhaps. There appears
to be a fault in the frame
I have been lived into.

Something right?

Never. Only almost
when you do not notice
something wrong.

.

And for my last trick I

Patriot

Oh flower of Scotland
there's something wrong
with the moater.

.

Pat riot?

Pait rot?

What am I
doing
here?

.

Pink petals
float

over the green
lawn

where birds sing
spring

and you call this
Glasgow?

Often I find myself stopped
before this point as I
can’t justify the words

yet I don’t think there is
any difference between that
and this, but one exists.

Leaves point
light back.

Why can’t I
do that.

.

The lion is tamed
in my wildest dream
and wears a 3-piece-flute.

.

Stolen flares
out of fashion
he’s on fire
watch out

.

I am something
in the air

I opted out
after forty winks
the magician made the kitchen
sink dissipate but everything else
doubled, quadrupled, infinitied away
from where I buried my head.

.

My tearstub was jerked

at the movies
through the movies
I mean window

It is such an effort
to create, I screamed
under my breath
as the grass grew
over my dead body.

.

Over my dead body
I said to the fisherman
who hooked my cheek
& tossed me into the sea.

.

That wasn't so bad
now was it went
the doctor with his jag
who gave me a lift
to where just one of
everything exists.

We’ve been waiting for you

.

I’m not ready to come back
but they drop me off
and I am a bird
the rain
some mud

Can I come in?

20.05.10 (earlier)

Exclusive

By Norman Silvester

Rangers keeper
James McGregor
has been told

he won't be charged
by police sex
attack probe

*

Different types
of memory
make marks

from the trip
the tip of your shoe
stings your ankle

you stumble into the past

familiar in its strangeness

like the snail, its slow trail
more graceful than the rhythm
of a distant shuffle

you read the people
as they walk past
eyes fixed firm
ahead, straight
ahead

Is the Beast weighing me down I shivered earlier

and heard things

said things too

felt them

you know

recognised

There is the visual memory
the audio level
taste & smell
even feel

and then there's that thing in your head
- "that's you" - in stages

the orange light flickers through the leaves
and it is right there, my lowdown universe

more drama in the night, silent
thoughtful, strange

remember that?

20.05.10 (later)

You've got to go in
to drop out

and this is it, this is
not it   do you know

what I mean is this
place where dialogue rises and
falls - there is a shift

the atmosphere switches
the sound of the room
becomes the wind
with someone else's monsters
among the trees & what
do you believe? Close
your eyes and look

then come back

The fox
is chased
by the shadow
of a fox
in my eye.

.

Quiet out
you can hear
yourself
here

because it's Wednesday night
that's right

Application

A number of inaccuracies
indicated the lack of an eye
for detail. You know what
unsuccessful means?

Applied
in another direction.

.

Deep down

I won't try
I can't try

.

How about we
relocate the world?

Good suggestion
but have you considered

the cost.

Let's put our heads
together tomorrow.

26.05.10 (Sides of Myself)

Envelope

The KEY Moments
occur in the past
& are validated
in the future.

Prove it.

Back there you had
the key right
(take a breath)
drink all the
licker

down in costa ricker
sings Blair in

his Southern
Glasgow
        drawl
& now the song
   has changed

It's everyday memory

But only when
   it's involuntary .

-- Can't force the muse
        which is the epiphany
                or key memory.

Music

is a different

sense of time

-- when you're in

it .

This

Place

Bill Summary and Detail

Glazer sends love

to you.

Love to you

Glazer.

Paul Stoller is a funny guy

a Salty Dog

Bay bay

Varying candles (perhaps I hate

familiarity - I do - that's true

- I am convinced

this is true

- Do you

believe me?

How do you *hear* language.

Language? No silence

ever.

*

Full

stop .

Stop

Time is sort of important

Napkins

- So I hear you can’t
  bear to (get distracted -

the voice is gone -
- Jesus shivers
  complex angles
  on river road

Welcome!
- You saw that shelf
- What *is* a shelf
- Really....

- My eye on a
journey - inside
behind
my eye
on a journey
Write: Here

(this place - this
piece of soft
tissue)

goes

Prayers

these words

strange on my tongue

as I go deeper

get con-fused

*

What they are attached to

I can't quite see

but feel

still you can shake yourself

into anything

*

& there's a tune

playing in my head

& there's a tune

playing

in my

head

& (even louder

as he writes)

[the past] Shape

yourself

That was when he met (named) Shiver

his private beast that laid eggs.

Looking at this forest you wonder

girl put down that comic

& her mother's eyes

were bigger then - you see?

Why Do You Have To Be 'The Best'?

There was I tripping
    (where I was tipping

            the   ash

                                    cloud

Images (<u>visual</u>)

in some order

(& he rubs his eyes

& spins

So this is the film

- me writing this

you watching this

US MAKING <u>this</u>

(tap tap tap

hand full
of contradictions

a world
full
of complications

The Blinking Moon

starring Frank Frink and Willie Singerman

as

frankfrink24 and williesingerman

Frank: considering changing my identity

Willie: me too

F: this is reality is it not

W: is this not?

F: is THIS not?

W: not

F: not no-one is BUYING

W: ring for a change of tone

frankfrink24

Cutoff. Oh well back to me on this here island. Done, dusted, your board, right you're bored, right? Speak who language now

Whoever in charge at this moment, to use a technological metaphor, ha ha a pompous buzz around my Moustache why the capitals? Synchronise

Your watches now who is catching up - live, a moment, see you layer! Says the statue of lord Morrison that superman sorry Market owner, or

Perhaps Uncle of, we'll see : funny round this world goes round your eyes, it's little about the sound now slow down son, it's just the blin

King moon. Good night

27.05.10 (Time Travels)

What can I say?

*

Everything has a face.

*

Caution

Biological hazard

How's my driving?

There is a certain impulse
I will obey
        Wherever I am
Notwithstanding
Sitting
Among other conversation
And my
Life is not something
I can give meaning to you
Other
I am unable to explain myself
On terms you get
And it tears me
Up really it does
Tho it seems tears are made
In spaces familiar, allowed
But this is not the place

Just too much (de

Sometimes the off-licence
Is a pet store, the wasteland
An eyesore, where people are piled
And put their feet up on balconies
To admire motorways

liberate

It's ok

My heart is quite big

*

Change decodes

A lot of me

What colour is your cage?

A series of voices

Yes a series of voices

Are we on the surface Fred?

I don't know Anne.

Keep moving

Down

Of course

Deeper right is this

Oh.   Wait

Fine it's fine

We’ll take a breath

Well take a breath

We'll rake abreadth

Real wake abridge

Riverrun

Rum and measles

All a sudden you can call me
Pugwash, the avocado baby
In the library the memory empty
At the time now refilled & more
Revealed, ah yes now goes on like
Those vibrations - something stops
Buzzing ah yes my back is relaxed
I don't think about much much
You see

I hope you have filled me in.

For me, death is a tree
Don't ask me why
I see it
Death is a tree

*

Boomerang
In the cellar

*

Seems to me
It can all come out
In a bad way
Or a good way

Though it's not either/or

*

Strange zipping noise
Upstairs

No louder now
Not sure where
Sounds like static

Wired

*

Weird to be nearly
alone in Blair's flat
round midnight

I exist
At this roundabout
Through
And across
This circle

Look out
For one way
Streets
Like lampposts and an unbalanced shoe
Once
Again

I am genuinely here

Riverford Road

Blind river

Sauv blan

Red lights

Beeps stop

Bird peeps

Peeps my feet the leaves

Look up on time (familiar)

Another direction from the toll

Cross my loof & hope to die

These are the newlands now

I haven't boarded up & down this hill

In years (time does pass

Look up I'm going slow

Peeping riverside road

White lines the postbox is

Red, says WED for some reason

And new people live on this street

And you actually see them now and

Again I voiced my fear of being that strange guy

Wondering up and down

Only kidding of course

And Blair says you'll be the new
Birdie man I'm laughing for ages
Sometimes recording bothers me some
Times not knot tho. Evenly spaced
Amber streetlamps - I accept them ok
The words implied behind the association is fine
The association is between thought and image
With language implied, untranslatable

Into a language impossible
I am trying to translate
Into theirs and there were smiles
In my mind, powerful feelings real
Hard saying this you know I feel
The weight of the world is my head

Last few steps, few deep breaths

Newlands

Are the boys still competing
over who has the biggest
piece of cake?

Not me, repeats
Sammy over
and over again he says

Don't make me take
another and yet
who was there

when the world was fair,
a young maiden, her hair
faded to gold and the sunset

These treats that make you feel
five years old and then

sickly five years old
sickly-six years of age

and this world is not
from concentrate

this world is full of marsh
mallows, so hollow they are
100% extra free fat free

My throat is sticky, my ears
aren't clear, the plague
has met my teeth

and the birds keep peeping
my jogging memory

these rise and falling thoughts, those
angelswept clouds over riverran

And Malcolm Mooney's there, you know
I stole an amber light for him it elegantly
faded, or was it urgently? It's hard to re-
member, sure nothing was left are you
outside the door there was a cold telephone
with an imaginary line and those felt-tipped
shapes that spelled those permanent words
this land is your land and my land

ourland is nowhere

Frink in the afternoon

The sun is shining in this world in my eye, nevermind
passwords, money, shadows, certain beasts, uncertain beats,
random bets - this will

Make sense, I hold this moment under my arm like a
magazine, a bridge, a grey cloud, traffic, changing places,
signs, mirrors, rivers & so

On a patch of sunlight, sweet nothing, wondering in
whatever world you wish, almost or somehow, somedown,
watch out crossing roads. Hi, life

You Call This The End

i said this is where i store my heart
without words it was not something
to impress, no, i stress i did not say
it, anything at all, but you know
how these hypnothermal situations
gather round us at times, surely someone
can relate to this hand outstretched -

28.05.10

I have your heart
in my head (will you
get it) my meaning is trying
to squeeze through your ears

hear me now
                    the moon won't bloom
any bigger
                    after the weekend
    into June

.

At least the trees will be
green, thank God for that I
counted my blessings but they
became sheep, put me to sleep
merrily, terribly, merrily,
dream is but a life

About

A W Singerman is also known as Willie Singerman, a singer-songwriter. He relocated from London to Glasgow whilst writing 'May' and has since moved back. Find out more at

www.williesingerman.com